AUSTRALIA UNCOVERED

jeremy

Published in Australia by
Weldon Kids Pty Ltd
1 /565 Willoughby Road, Willoughby NSW 2068, Australia
A member of the Weldon International Group of Companies
First published 1993   First reprint 1993

Publisher: Leonie Weldon
Project Co-ordinator & Promotions: Leah Walsh
Managing Editor: Avril Janks
Designer: Astri Baker
Production Manager: Cathy Wadling
Printed by Australian Print Group

All illustrations by Jeremy Pty Limited 1993

National Library Cataloguing-in-Publication data:
Australia Uncovered.

ISBN 1 86302 300 3.

1. Australia - Juvenile Literature. I Andrew, Jeremy

994
Researchers/Editors
Margaret McFee
Linsay Knight
Dimity MacDonald

Everything under the
Southern Cross. Odds & Sods,
bits and bobs. All you didn't
think you wanted to know about.
A pleasurable exploration
of our beloved country.
A question of facts.
Tell your friends to buy one too.
An unputdownable guide
to the sunburnt country.

WELDON
KiDS

Helpful people and organisations we would like to thank **Cara Badger** Frank Fogliati **Mary Jane Giekie** Terry Lindsey **Belinda, Benjamin and Jamie Peel** Damian Tenze **The Publisher's brother Harold** The Publisher's dad • **ACT Tourist Commission** Australia Post **Australian Department of Administrative Services** Australian Electoral Commission **Black Books** Bureau of Meteorology **Bureau of Statistics** Bureau of Tourism Research **Bushfire Council** Chicken Growers Association **Department of Mineral Resources** Geo Magazine **Gerald to Greenough Travel Centre** Hydrographic Department of the Royal Australian Navy **Macquarie Library Pty Ltd** National Parks and Wildlife Service **Netball Association of Australia** New South Wales Fisheries **New South Wales Tourist Commission** Northern Suburbs Basketball Association **Northern Territory Tourism Corporation** Queensland Tourism and Travel Corporation **Roads and Traffic Authority (NSW)** State Library of New South Wales **State Rail** Telecom Australia Directory Assistance **Tourism South Australia Travel Centre** Tourism Victoria **Western Australia Tourist Centre** All the hundreds of people who put us through to another department

Contents

Wild Australia

▲

Introducing Australia

Although Australia is the world's largest island, it is also the smallest and least populated continent in the world.

Our island nation is the oldest, flattest, lowest, driest and most isolated continent. One-fifth of Australia is desert and two-thirds is arid and thus not much better than desert. Most Australians cling to the coast, making the centre very empty.

Australia is the sixth largest country in the world, with an area of 7,682,300 square km, including Tasmania. Taking up almost six per cent of the world's land surface, Australia is almost as big as the United States. Great Britain would fit into Australia about 30 times and Japan would fit about 20 times.

To give some idea of the vast distances involved when travelling across Australia, think about this fact. The distance between Perth and Adelaide of around 3,000 km (not even the whole way from the west to the east of Australia) is about the same as the distance between London and Moscow.

▲

A Big Country with a Big Backyard

The official distance around the Australian coast, including Tasmania, is 36,735 km. If you walked non-stop for 24 hours a day around the coast, including all the bays, harbours, inlets, capes and promontories, you would cover nearly four times this distance. Besides being exhausted, you would have walked 136,000 km and been away from home for about three years and 36 days.

MIRAGE...

Pick a card!

My eyes are playing tricks on me...

21 Facts to Stun your Friends

- •• **The largest city** – Sydney,
  with a population of 3,700,000

- •• **Most northerly point** – Cape York
  in Queensland

- •• **Most southerly point** – South East Cape
  in Tasmania

- •• **Most easterly point**
  – Cape Byron
  in New South Wales

- •• **Most westerly point**
  – Steep Point in
  Western Australia

- •• **Greatest distance
  from west to east**
  –4,000 km

- •• **Greatest distance
  from north to south**
  – 3,680 km

- •• **Highest point**
  – Mount Kosciusko
  in New South Wales
  (2,229 m)

- •• **Lowest point** – the south end of Lake Eyre
  (11 m below sea level)

- •• **Longest mountain range** – The Great Divide
  (3,620 km from northern Queensland to
  South Australia)

- •• **Biggest desert** – Great Sandy Desert
  in Western Australia (414,000 square km,
  six times the area of Tasmania)

▲

- •• **Australia's deserts (in size order)** – Great Sandy Desert, Great Victorian Desert, Simpson Desert, Tanami Desert, Little Sandy Desert, Gibson Desert, Sturts Stony Desert, Tirari Desert, Strzelecki Desert

- •• **Longest river** – Murray-Darling-Culgoa-Balonne-Condamine River (3,750 km)

- •• **Largest natural lake** – The Great Lake in Tasmania (25 km long and 5 to 8 km wide)

- •• **Deepest lake** – Lake St Clair in Tasmania (200 m deep)

- •• **Highest waterfall** – Wollomombi Falls in New South Wales (a series of falls 334 m long. The longest single fall is 200 m, which is about the same height as the BP sign on top of Bourke Place in Melbourne – now isn't that interesting?)

- •• **Largest bay** – The Great Australian Bight (1,110 km long)

- •• **Largest island** – Tasmania (67,896 square km)

- •• **Number of islands** – named, 1,267; unnamed, countless

- •• **Longest place names** – Lake Cadibarrawirracanna in South Australia and Lake Mirranpongapongunna in Queensland

- •• **Other great place names** – Warralillialillialillia – South Australia Boomahnoomoonha – Victoria Moombooldool – New South Wales Indooroopilly – Queensland

The Great Australian
Bight ...

Yonks Away

Australia, in the Southern Hemisphere, is a very long way from England and the rest of Europe, where our first white settlers came from. Flying distance from Sydney to London is about 17,000 km; from Sydney to New York it's about 16,000 km, and even New Zealand is about 2,000 km away.

The People of Australia

Aussies, a Rare Breed?

In June 1990 the total population for the whole of Australia was 17,086,197 (about 17 million people). Even though the average number of people per square km is 2.2, most Australians actually live on the coast, making the edges densely populated and the centre very empty!

Compared to many other countries we have plenty of room to move. In Hong Kong there are 5,436 people for every square kilometre, while the USA has 26 people and Britain 234 for the same area.

Aboriginal Australians

Australia is the country of the Aboriginal people. Like all indigenous people around the world, they have a close affinity with the land and have never tried to control it, considering themselves part of it. They can survive on the land as no other people can. The plants, animals and landforms of Australia all have an important place in their lives, and their history is taught to new generations of Aboriginal people through songs, paintings and stories. The Aboriginal population is increasing and at the last census was 1.5 per cent of the Australian population, although not all the Aboriginal people take part in the census.

The Flag

The Aboriginal flag, designed by Harold Thomas, was first flown only in 1971. The black stands for the

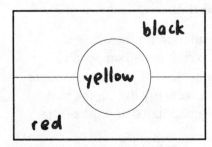

Aboriginal people, the yellow represents the sun, the giver of life, and the red is the colour of the earth and the blood that has been shed. Please colour the flag in.

Bushfood and Medicine

Aboriginal people have had their knowledge of bushfoods and medicines almost longer than time itself, and were living on a varied, tasty and balanced diet of fruits, nuts, roots, vegetables meats and fish before Europeans came to Australia. As their whole existence was dependent on the land, this is where they also found their medicines. Tea-tree oil is sold commercially and is very popular with Australians. Its antiseptic and antifungal properties were discovered, and used for hundreds of years, by the Aboriginal people. They used medicine from plants or herbs for every ailment - anything from bandages of wattle bark for headaches to crushed orchid seeds for dressing spear wounds. Some Aboriginal people still live in traditional communities and use these remedies, while others live in urban society.

Bush Tucker fast food

Immigrant in Australia discovers the roots of his family tree...

The Torres Strait Islanders

The Torres Strait Islands are directly north of Cape York Peninsula, Queensland, and are a group of about 100 islands. Only 18 of the islands are inhabited. Also indigenous people, the Islanders have different cultural backgrounds and traditions to the mainland Aboriginal people.

The Flag

The Torres Strait Islands flag was recently designed by Bernard Namok of Thursday Island. It features a white traditional dancing headdress and a five-pointed white star, representing the five island groups. There are green stripes for the land, blue stripes for the sea and black stripes for the people. Please colour in the flag.

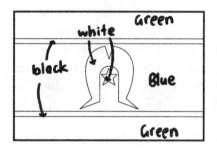

The Immigrants

All Australians bar the Aboriginal people came here as immigrants. If you're not Aboriginal, find out your family's history - did your parents, grandparents, great-grandparents or great-great grandparents first come here to live from another country? Australia is proud to be a multicultural society.

People have come from countries all over the world to live in Australia. These are just some of the places immigrants come from: England, Ireland, Scotland, Germany, Italy, Greece, Holland, Malta, China, Japan, various states in Africa, Poland, Lebanon, Vietnam, India, Turkey, Yugoslavia and New Zealand.

Having a nation made up of many nationalities has meant we have a wonderful mix of talents, music, art, traditions and religions, and hundreds of delicious foods to choose from. There are food names we are all familiar with which are now part of our language, as the food is part of our diet. Mr Macquarie, the Australian dictionary man himself, has given us some examples and origins.

- ••• fetta (cheese) from Greece
- ••• fettuccine from Italy
- ••• hamburger from Germany
- ••• nachos from Mexico
- ••• tabouli from Turkey and Lebanon
- ••• schnitzel from Austria
- ••• quiche from France
- ••• satay and samoosa from Asia

World Famous

Australian Made

America has the Grand Canyon, Japan has Mount Fuji and Australia has Uluru and the Great Barrier Reef. Both of these are in the list of the eight World Heritage areas in our country.

Uluru National Park

Formerly called Ayers Rock, Uluru is the largest monolith in the country and is a very sacred site to the Aboriginal people. It is 2.5 km long, 1.6 km wide and 9.4 km around its base, covers 3.33 square km and rises 348 m above the surrounding desert. Geologists believe that, like an iceberg, only about one-sixth of the rock's true mass protrudes above the ground. More than 75,000 people attempt to walk to the top every year.

The Great Barrier Reef...
School of tourist fish view the wildlife in a glass-top boat...

The Great Barrier Reef

The Great Barrier Reef is the largest and most spectacular coral reef in the world. Stretching from Fraser Island off the Bundaberg coast in Queensland all the way up to the Papua New Guinean coastline, the Reef is about 2,300 km long. It covers an area of about 200,000 square km, and includes 700 islands. More than 1,500 species of fish are known to live in the reef region and half of these types may occur on a single reef!

The other six World Heritage areas are:

- •• The Lord Howe Island Group in New South Wales
- •• Kakadu National Park in Northern Territory
- •• Willandra Lakes Region in New South Wales
- •• Tasmanian Wilderness
- •• The Australian East Coast temperate and subtropical Rainforest Parks in New South Wales and Queensland
- •• The Wet Tropics of Queensland

When part of a country has been chosen, the nation responsible has to promise to ensure the Heritage area's "identification, protection, conservation, presentation and transmission to future generations ... to the utmost of its own resources".

Australian Man-made

Paris has the Eiffel Tower, London has Big Ben, New York has the Statue of Liberty – and Australia has its own world famous man-made landmarks.

Sydney Opera House

The Sydney Opera House stands proudly on Bennelong Point, and has become the most famous building in Australia. This unusual structure was designed by the Danish architect Joern Utzon, who resigned before it was completed. Although its shape reminds the onlooker of the yachts that skim past it daily, Utzon always said that he was inspired by the curved segments of an orange.

where the inspiration for the Bridge came from...

Sydney Harbour Bridge

Opened on 19 March 1932, the Sydney Harbour Bridge is the largest bridge in Australia and the third largest steel arch bridge in the world. Weighing in at 52,732 tonnes, with a span of 503 m or half a kilometre, the bridge creates a vital link between the northern and southern parts of the city.

Businessman working in Australia's tallest building catches the 8.45 Cloud to work...

The Biggest

Tall Storeys

The 60 storey MLC office tower in Sydney is Australia's tallest building. It rises to a height of 242 m and was completed in 1985.

The Longest Bridge

The $220 million West Gate Bridge in Melbourne is Australia's longest. Its overall length is 2,582.57 m, with a river span of 336 m.

King Koala visits
Centrepoint Tower
from the outside...

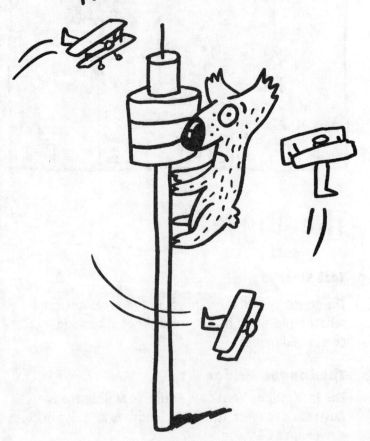

Best View in Town

Centrepoint Tower is our highest observation tower. It stands 304.8 m above the street and can hold 960 people. The elevators zip up and down the tower at 25.6 km per hour, so hold on to your stomach!

If you don't like lifts, you can always take the stairs, like Maurice Angania. He set the record for climbing the tower's 1,370 steps in June 1986, when he made it to the top in only seven minutes and 29 seconds!

I've Never Heard of it Either

The BP logo on top of Bourke Place in Melbourne is Australia's highest sign. The building, completed in 1991, towers 224 m above the ground and is 48 storeys high.

Holy Heights

Australia's tallest church is St Patrick's Cathedral in Melbourne. The 103 m high spire has been standing majestically since 1937.

A Pole Apart

The stately 81 m high flagpole topping Parliament House in Canberra is Australia's tallest flagpole. It is made of stainless steel and was erected just before the building was officially opened in 1988.

So What?

The 426.7 m high Omega Navigational Mast is our tallest structure. It was erected in Gippsland, Victoria in 1983.

The Big Syndrome

Across our nation there are scattered bizarre man-made structures that have become major tourist attractions. Look out for them as you travel across Australia – you can't miss them. Here are some of our favourites.

The Big Banana

This enormous piece of cement fruit may be found at Coff's Harbour in New South Wales. It was built about 30 years ago.

The Big Pineapple

If you like your fruit big, why not visit the giant pineapple that stands in the midst of a plantation on the Sunshine Coast in Queensland?

The Big Merino

This giant sheep is to be found at Goulburn in New South Wales. It is 15 m wide and 18 m high. There are shops to visit and you can find out all about growing wool. When you visit, don't forget that you can look though the sheep's eyes.

Larry the Lobster

This amazing creature is made out of chicken wire, hessian, foam and fibreglass. Inside, there is an aquarium and a theatre screening films about lobster fishing. So have a look at Larry if you're ever in Kingston in South Australia.

The Giant Worm

What about a day at a worm-shaped museum? This one celebrates the longest worm to be found in Australia. This species of worm, Megascolides australis (pronounced meg-uh-skol-ee-dees os-trah-luhs), sometimes grows up to 3 m in length. You can see the Giant Worm in Bass, Victoria, where the real-life giant earthworms live as well.

More we've Heard of

- ••• The Big Cow
- ••• The Big Bottle
- ••• The Big Frost
- ••• The Big Oyster

If you've heard of others, please let us know.

A Look at the Weather

Australians only ever talk about the weather in terms of summer and winter, as we don't have dramatic changes between the four seasons. Our native trees are evergreen and snow falls only in minute parts of the country.

A land as big as Australia can experience all types of weather.

11 Climatic Facts to Bore your Friends

- •• **Hottest place** - Marble Bar in Western Australia (average summer temperature 41°C)
- •• **Coldest places** - Mount Perisher and Mount Crackenback, in New South Wales
- •• **Windiest city** - Perth in Western Australia (average wind speed 15.6 km/h)
- •• **Wettest place** - Tully in Queensland (average rainfall 4.3 m per year)
- •• **Most rainy days a year** - 314 on average, at Waratah in Tasmania
- •• **Highest rainfall** - 11.251 mm, in 1979, at Bellenden Kerr in Queensland
- •• **Driest place** - the Lake Eyre area in South Australia (average annual rainfall below 100 mm)
- •• **Longest heatwave** - 161 days, at Marble Bar in Western Australia (1923-24)
- •• **Foggiest city** - Canberra (average of 47 days per year)
- •• **Coldest day recorded** - -22.2°C, at Charlotte's Pass in New South Wales on 14 July 1945 and 22 August 1947
- •• **Hottest day recorded** - 53.1°C, at Cloncurry in Queensland on 16 January 1889

Too Hot for Pencils

In 1845 the explorer Charles Sturt claimed to have recorded a temperature of 57.2°C at Cooper Creek in south-west Queensland. It was so hot, he declared, that the lead dropped out of his pencils!

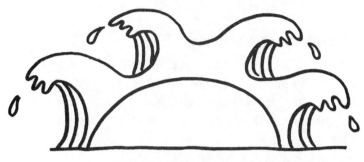

HEATWAVE ...

Mother Nature Gets Tough

Widespread floods occur more often in the northern and eastern coastal areas of the country. As a land of extremes, Australia has also suffered nine major droughts since the 1860s.

Cyclone Tracy

The infamous Cyclone Tracy struck Darwin on Christmas morning 1974. With wind speeds of up to 300 km/h, 50 people were killed, 16 were reported missing and more than 30,000 were evacuated.

Nyngan Floods

When floods hit the town of Nyngan in New South Wales in April 1990, the population of 2,200 had to be evacuated. The waters rose from floor to ceiling height in just two hours!

Buaraba Creek Hailstorm

A severe hailstorm hit Buaraba Creek near Lowood in Queensland on 1 January 1969. Hailstones forming drifts of up to 4 m deep left cattle embedded in ice! More than 200 cattle were killed and there was widespread damage to crops.

Don't Move to Willeton!

On 17 September 1974, Willeton, a suburb of Perth, experienced a severe electrical storm. Two people speaking on the telephone were knocked unconscious when lightning hit the lines they were using. In the same year on 13 November the same thing happened to another Willeton resident.

Strike One

At the Latrobe sportsground in Tasmania on 24 May 1975, 50 people were hit by lightning. Amazingly, only one person was seriously injured.

Our Seasons

- •• Spring starts 1 September
- •• Summer starts 1 December
- •• Autumn starts 1 March
- •• Winter starts 1 June

We've Golden Soil and Wealth for Toil...

Under the Surface

Mining has been and will continue to be a part of
Australia's economic wealth. We earn more in exporting
minerals than we do from agriculture. We produce more
diamonds and export more coal than any other country
in the world. But the protection of our precious
environment should always be considered before we
automatically take from our sometimes fragile and
special places.

The Top Ten Mining Products

- ••• Alumina
- ••• Bauxite
- ••• Mineral sands
- ••• Iron
- ••• Nickel
- ••• Gold
- ••• Copper
- ••• Natural gas
- ••• Oil
- ••• Uranium

Opal!

Australia produces 95 per cent of the world's fine opal. This represents about $106 million dollars a year in revenue.

On the Land

It used to be said that Australia rode on the sheep's back, because so much of our wealth came from wool. Mining has now overtaken agriculture as our major export, due to world price wars and increases in mining production.

Our Aussie farmers working on the land often find life tough as Australia is the driest continent in the world (not counting Antarctica). Our life-giving artesian water must be counted as the most valuable resource to come out of the ground of Australia.

Farmer Bruce camps overnight on his property during a routine walk to his mailbox...

Largest Property

The largest property in Australia is Anna Creek in South Australia, which is 30,113.5 square km – that's nearly half the size of Tasmania and about the same size as The Netherlands.

IRRITABULL...

Cattle caught in traffic jam begin blowing their horns...

Livestock

We are lucky in Australia as there is no need to import food to survive, and we have a wide variety of meats, from veal to venison. Our farmers have a big job looking after these guys: we have about 22 million cattle, 162 million sheep, 3 million pigs and 57 million chickens in Australia.

Crops

Two per cent of our country's land mass is planted with crops.

Top Crops

- •• Wheat
- •• Barley
- •• Oats
- •• Sorghum
- •• Maize
- •• Rice
- •• Rye
- •• Millet
- •• Lots of vegetables
- •• Lots of fruit

Wild Australia

Dinosaurs

During the Triassic and Jurassic periods 225 million to 135 million years ago, Australia was ruled by dinosaurs. The Rhaetosaurus and the Austrasaurus were both harmless, four-legged, plant-eating dinosaurs that grew to a length of about 15 m.

The slightly smaller megalosaurus was a little more intimidating. It was a two-legged flesh-eating predator that grew to a length of approximately 12 m.

And if you think it was safer to stick to the water, plesiosaur Kronosaurus queenslandicus and Ichythyosaus australias were both huge swimming, dinosaur-sized reptiles.

After the dinosaurs died out about 65 million years ago, there were no large land animals in Australia for over 60 million years. Then it was time for the giant mammals to have their millennium. The giant Kangaroo was over 3 m high, while the Diprotodon (oversized ancestor of the Wombat) was as big as a rhinoceros! Archaeologists have also found evidence of a very nasty-looking Tasmanian Wolf.

Unique Creatures of Australia

This country is rich in wildlife. An island continent, Australia has been isolated to an unusual degree from other continents for many millions of years. This has given us unique plants and animals, many of which are found only in Australia. The groovy scientific name for this is "endemic". Koalas, for example, are only found here, and are therefore endemic, whereas cassowaries are also found in New Guinea, and therefore aren't endemic – you've got it!

To learn about Australia's wildlife, let's start with the basics.

- ••• A **mammal** is a hairy or furry animal that feeds its young with milk from the mother's teats.

- ••• A **marsupial** is a type of mammal where the females have pouches, in which they raise their young.

- ••• A **monotreme** is an unusual type of **mammal**, only found in Australia and Papua New Guinea, whose young hatch from eggs. The echidna and the platypus are monotremes.

- ••• A **reptile** is a coldblooded animal with a backbone, and a dry, scaly skin.

- ••• An **amphibian** is an animal that lives both on land and in water. It has a backbone too, but its skin is often damp and slimy.

Confused? Now try this one. Groups of animals or plants – say, the kangaroos or the eucalypts – are divided into

Modern Australian animals keeping up with the changing times...

Young urban echidna sports a new flat-top haircut...

Yuppie roo finds a place for his mobile phone...

Daredevil platypus saves up for a jet ski ...

Sporty emu discovers in-line skating..

species. Each species is a different type of animal or plant in that group. For example, the Western grey kangaroo is a species of kangaroo, and the scribbly bark gum is a species of eucalypt.

Australia has:

- about 230 species of mammals
- about 750 species of birds
- about 700 species of reptiles
- about 140 species of frogs
- about 181 species of freshwater fish
- about 3,000 species of marine fish
- about 65,000 species of insects

Here are Australia's Most Popular Animals

- Kangaroo
- Koala
- Echidna
- Frill-necked lizard
- Emu
- Cockatoo
- Dingo
- Numbat
- Tasmanian devil
- Kookaburra
- Sugar-glider
- Rainbow lorikeet
- Brush-tail possum
- Platypus

Frill-necked Lizard...

Here are some Interesting Animal Facts for People who Don't Find Animals Interesting

Star of the Cage

The world-famous budgerigar is a native Australian parrot. Wild budgies are green and gold, smaller than the pet breeds, and can be seen in the arid interior in huge flocks. In the 1840s, the budgie was a hot item in London, selling for more than an average worker could earn in a year.

A Snake with a Sting

Gram for gram, the inland taipan has the most potent venom of all the snakes in the world. A bite from this creature would be quite likely to kill a human being. Fortunately, the inland taipan is a relatively shy and placid snake, unlikely to attack a human unless attacked or provoked.

Ancient Queens

Scientists believe that the Australian insects with the longest life span are the queens of one particular species of termite. It was reported that one Queensland queen was still breeding 63 years after being found in 1872.

Big Builders

While on the subject of termites, look out for termite workers in eastern parts of Australia. They have been known to construct mounds to a height of 6.1 m, measuring 31 m around the base. If termites were the same size as us, their dwellings would be five times as high as Centrepoint Tower (this measures a mighty 304 m).

Speedsters on the Wing

One of the fastest fliers in the insect world is one species of Australian dragonfly. A speed of 98.6 km per hour (ground speed) was recorded in 1917 over a distance of about 82 m. Most dragonflies can fly up to about 57 km per hour.

Beware of the Spider

Sydneysiders are always wary of our most venomous spider, the funnelweb, which has been responsible for 12 recorded deaths since 1927. Funnelwebs normally live in burrows in the ground, but they can wander into houses if their burrows are flooded out in wet weather or disturbed by building. Unlike most spiders, funnelwebs

are extremely aggressive, and quite likely to bite if provoked. Fortunately, an effective anti-venene (antidote to the poison) and also bricks, spades, Macquarie Dictionaries, pieces of 4 by 2 and Dad's golfing trophies are readily available, and in recent years few people have died from bites by the funnelweb.

Hi-tech Mammal

Most creatures, humans included, use sound and vision as a means of obtaining information about the world around them. But some animals use far more subtle methods. When the platypus searches underwater for food, it relies very little on its sight or hearing, using its sensitive snout instead. This has sensors that can pick up the minute electrical signals coming from the nervous systems of all animals. Using these signals, the platypus can work out the size, direction of movement and distance of its dinner.

A Mysterious Bird

The night parrot has the scientists who study nature scratching their heads. This bird is so secretive that it is almost impossible to observe it. It is active only at night, spending the day deep within clumps of spinifex grass, where it is safe from almost any disturbance. When it is seen, it is seen by chance only, and that happens only about once or twice a decade. Almost nothing is known of the bird's behaviour, numbers or where it lives – or even if it really is an endangered animal.

We Don't Have a Grizzly Bear ...

But we do have the bulldog ant, the world's most primitive ant. It is also one of the biggest ants in the world. When it attacks people, it uses its sting and jaws at the same time, causing great pain. The results are seldom very serious, but this ant is known to have killed at least three people.

the neighbourhood bully takes his giant bulldog ant, Fido, for a walk...

Don't Tell Mum I Ate the Kids

The gastric-brooding frog has one of the strangest breeding cycles of all the frog species in the world. This small frog lives (or lived - see 'Absent Amphibians' on **p.54**) along streams in the rainforests of eastern Queensland. The female lays about 25 eggs and then swallows them, and they end up in her stomach. The tadpoles excrete a substance that prevents the mother's stomach from digesting them, so they can live there safely for about six weeks. Once they are developed enough to venture into the world, they hop out through the mother's mouth - gross!

A Fishy Story

The largest Australian freshwater fish is the Murray Cod, which grows to a maximum weight of about 113 kg. The females lay up to 60,000 eggs at a time, which sink to the bottom and hatch after one to two weeks. Some Murray Cod are thought to reach as much as 50 or 60 years of age.

Sharks

Aaaaargh!! See page 110. ▶ ▶ ▶

Some of our Most Endangered Species

Like animals all over the world, a great number of Australia's native animals have had to struggle to survive. Humans have moved into areas that once were their habitats, bringing with them building developments and urban sprawl. These changes to the landscape have brought pollution, habitat degradation and the introduction of foreign animals, which are now feral pests. So many native Australian animals are in difficulties that it's hard to know which to mention. Here are some particularly sad cases.

Middle aged
hairy-nosed
   wombat...

...with
toupée

Mammals at Risk

Many researchers have given up all hope that the thylacine (Tasmanian tiger) is still surviving, while the pig-footed bandicoot hasn't been seen since the 1920s. And the hairy-nosed wombat survives only in a single small reserve in tropical Queensland. Even though this creature is the faunal (animal) emblem of South Australia, there are no more of its kind in this state.

Threatened Birds

The most famous of Australia's endangered bird species is certainly the night parrot, but because it is difficult to see it means we can't be sure if this bird really is endangered. Meanwhile, several other species have very small populations and are gravely threatened. The noisy scrub-bird numbers less than 200 individuals, which are confined to a couple of tiny reserves near Two Peoples Bay, Western Australia. Similarly, the orange-bellied parrot now numbers less than 500 birds, breeding only in remote south-western Tasmania and migrating to spend the winter along the Victorian coast around Port Philip Bay.

Absent Amphibians

So little is known about many Australian frogs that it is difficult to know whether some are endangered or just not seen very often. But there are a number of frog species that seem to be extremely rare and perhaps endangered. Thorough searches for the extraordinary gastric-brooding frog have all been unsuccessful since

around 1980. This frog is now feared to be extinct. The Eungella torrent-frog and one or two other Queensland rainforest frogs have also disappeared.

Rare Reptiles

The most critically endangered of all Australian reptiles is the Western swamp tortoise. This tortoise is restricted to a single wetland near Perth, and its wild population is now reduced to an estimated 20 individuals. The Perth Zoo has a small captive colony, and a breeding and restocking program is being carried out.

Find the Fish

The trout (or bluenosed) cod, once widespread in rivers of the Murray-Darling system, is now restricted to the upper reaches of the Murray River in north-eastern Victoria. Its numbers are decreasing due to disease, the degradation of its habitat, overfishing, and competition from introduced trout.

Other threatened or vulnerable Australian freshwater fish include the Lake Eacham rainbowfish, found only in Lake Eacham on the Atherton Tableland; the saddled galaxias of central Tasmania, and the honey blue-eye, found only in a few small rivers in south-eastern Queensland.

Wanted ... Dead not Alive: Feral Pests

Australia's animals are unique due mainly to their isolation. When Europeans introduced foreign animals they had no idea of the immense destruction they would cause. Our country's animals, which took millions of years to develop to their present form, are now fighting for their lives against these recent invaders.

Small endangered marsupial under attack from a squadron of feral pigs...

Feral Cat

- **Estimated population:** ten million
- **Damage:** Directly responsible for the decline in native small mammals and birds.

Feral Pig

- **Estimated population:** five to 11 million
- **Damage:** Erosion, destruction of pastoral land and crops, disease carriers.

Rabbit

- **Estimated population:** 200 million
- **Damage:** Serious erosion, devastation of pastoral land and crops.

Cane Toad

- **Estimated population:** impossible to guess because they breed so rapidly
- **Damage:** Due to their poison they endanger any animal that eats them.

Buffalo

- **Estimated population:** 80,000
- **Damage:** Disruption of nesting sites and fresh water springs.

Feral Goat

- **Estimated population:** five to seven million
- **Damage:** Destruction of bush and massive soil erosion.

Fox

- •• **Estimated population:** two to five million
- •• **Damage:** Responsible for the extinction of many small mammals.

The Dingo Fence

The dingo fence is 1.8 m high and stretches for 5,531 km. That makes it nearly four times as long as the Great Wall of China. It is found approximately 250 km north from Broken Hill – a five-hour drive. The dingo fence is also known as the border fence or, by those who live on it, "the nettin". Twenty-two people work along the fence. It starts off in Western Australia, then goes through South Australia, then New South Wales, then back to South Australia and New South Wales and into Queensland. The fence was built originally to keep out rabbits, but failed to do so, and the Government added to its height and called it a dingo-proof fence, hence the name.

Australia's Flora

Australia's flora gives our landscape its character. Gumtrees, or eucalypts, are found just about everywhere, except in extremely arid areas and deep rainforest areas. There are about 700 species. Our wattles are also abundant, as we have about 600 species.

Many Australian plants in the bush need bushfires. Unlike the North American pineforests, which are devastated after fire, the Australian forest grows again.

The seeds of many plants will only germinate, or in

some cases the seed pods will only open, after exposure to the heat of a fire. Soon after a fire the black scorched trees and bushes are seen with new bright green shoots ready to start the cycle again.

Bushfires occur often. Many common trees contain large amounts of inflammable oils, which seem to ensure the fires will burn well.

Here is a Random Selection of Well-known Australian Plants

- ••• Gumtree
- ••• Bottle brush
- ••• Tea tree
- ••• Lilly pilly
- ••• Banksia
- ••• Silky oak
- ••• Waratah
- ••• Wattle
- ••• Casuarina
- ••• Red cedar
- ••• Kangaroo paw
- ••• Native orchid
- ••• Grasstree

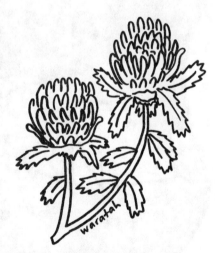
waratah

Swedish tourists splurge on luxurious 5 star accommodation

Official Stuff

Our National Anthem

"In joyful strains then let us sing" – wouldn't it be great if we all could do just that. The youth of Australia should take up the challenge and teach the rest of the nation our anthem!

Australians all let us rejoice,
For we are young and free,
We've golden soil and wealth for toil;
Our home is girt by sea;
Our land abounds in nature's gifts
Of beauty rich and rare,
In history's page, let every stage
Advance Australia Fair.
In joyful strains then let us sing,
Advance Australia Fair.

Beneath our radiant Southern Cross
We'll toil with hearts and hands;
To make this Commonwealth of ours
Renowned of all the lands;
For those who've come across the seas
We've boundless plains to share;
With courage let us all combine
To Advance Australia Fair.
In joyful strains then let us sing,
Advance Australia Fair.

What About a Flag?

The Australian flag features the British Union Jack against a blue background. A large seven-pointed star represents the six States and the Territories. The other five stars are the Southern Cross. (On a clear night, have a look at the stars and try to find the Southern Cross.)

As Australia gets closer to the day it becomes an independent republic, the pressure is increasing to change our flag's design. There is controversy over the flag, as many Australians would like the British Union Jack removed, and many new designs are always being suggested.

Our flag is well known. Find one, and then colour in our drawing to make it look official.

A yearning for our own identity is not new. Banjo Paterson, one of Australia's most famous writers and poets, wrote the poem on page 66 when he returned to Australia after fighting in the Anglo-Boer War for England under the English flag in 1900.

OUR OWN FLAG by Banjo Paterson

They mustered us up with a royal din,
In wearisome weeks of drought.
Ere ever the half of the crops were in,
Or the half of the sheds cut out.

'Twas down with saddle and spurs and whip
The swagman dropped his swag.
And we hurried us off to an outbound ship
To fight for the English flag.

The English flag - it is ours in sooth
We stand by it wrong or right.
But deep in our hearts is the honest truth
We fought for the sake of a fight.

And the English flag may flutter and wave
Where the World-wide Oceans toss,
But the flag the Australian dies to save
Is the flag of the Southern Cross.

If ever they want us to stand the brunt
Of a hard-fought, grim campaign,
We will carry our own flag up to the front
When we go to the wars again.

1900

The Commonwealth Coat of Arms

The Coat of Arms shows a kangaroo and an emu holding a shield. Above them is a seven-pointed star and behind is wattle, the national floral emblem.

Major Political Parties

It is the law that you must vote in elections once you are 18 years of age. The three major political parties in Australia are the Australian Labor Party, the Liberal Party and the National Party of Australia. After these comes the Australian Democrats, and after this come heaps many have never heard of, so we thought we'd take the opportunity to give them a plug.

1912, Kangaroo tries on the Australian Coat of Arms for size...

It fits!

List of All the Other Registered Political Parties

- Australian Shooters Party
- "Green" parties (16 in all)
- Australians Against Further Immigration
- Call to Australia (Fred Nile) Group
- Citizens Electoral Councils of Australia Group
- Democratic Labor Party of Australia
- Grey Power
- Independent EFF
- Janet Powell Independents' Network
- Natural Law Party
- Northern Territory Country Liberal Party
- Pensioner and Citizen Initiated Referendum Alliance
- Republican Party of Australia
- Rex Connor (Snr) Labor Party
- Socialist Party of Australia
- Tasmania Senate Team
- Tasmanian Independent Senator Brian Harradine Group
- The Confederate Action Party of Australia
- The Federal Party of Australia
- Torres United Party

A National Flower for Australia

It wasn't until 1988 that the golden wattle became Australia's official national flower. As well as decorating the coat of arms, it reflects Australia's national colours: green and gold.

Modern-day jolly swagman

Waltzing Matilda - the Song that always Chokes up the Old Folk

Banjo Paterson wrote the original version of "Waltzing Matilda", which often comes second only to the national anthem. Here is the version we sing today:

Once a jolly swagman camped by a billabong,
Under the shade of a coolibah tree,
And he sang as he watched and waited till his "billy" boiled,
"You'll come a-waltzing Matilda with me.
Waltzing Matilda, Waltzing Matilda,
You'll come a-waltzing Matilda with me,"

And he sang as he watched and waited till his "billy"
boiled,
"You'll come a-waltzing Matilda with me."

Down came a jumbuck to drink at the billabong,
Up jumped the swagman and grabbed him with glee,
And he sang as he shoved that jumbuck in his tucker bag,
"You'll come a-waltzing Matilda with me,
Waltzing Matilda, Waltzing Matilda,
You'll come a-waltzing Matilda with me,"
And he sang as he shoved that jumbuck in his tucker bag,
"You'll come a-waltzing Matilda with me."

Up rode the squatter, mounted on his thoroughbred,
Down came the troopers, one, two, three,
"Who's that jolly jumbuck you've got in your tucker bag?
You'll come a-waltzing Matilda with me."

Up jumped the swagman and sprang into the billabong,
"You'll never catch me alive," said he;
And his ghost may be heard as you pass by that billabong,
"You'll come a-waltzing Matilda with me,
Waltzing Matilda, Waltzing Matilda,
You'll come a-waltzing Matilda with me,"
And his ghost may be heard as you pass by that billabong,
"You'll come a-waltzing Matilda with me."

1895, first published 1903

▲

State by State

Australia's six
States of Mind...

JOYOUS — QLD.
REFINED — S.A.
PENSIVE — VIC.
CAREFREE — N.S.W.
BOLD — W.A.
ELUSIVE — TAS.

Australia is divided into six states and two territories.

The ACT

Australia's Capital Territory

- •• **Area Covered:** 2,359 square km,
  or about 0.03 per cent of Australia
- •• **Capital City:** Canberra
- •• **Longest River:** the Murrumbidgee River
- •• **Largest Lake:** Lake Burley Griffin
- •• **Highest Point:** Bimberi Peak (1,914 m)
- •• **Floral Emblem:** the Royal Bluebell
- •• **Faunal Emblem:** the Gang-Gang Cockatoo
- •• **Motto:** none

EXTRA TIDBITS AND ODDS AND SODS ON THE ACT

Canberra

Canberra is a planned, ordered, neat and tidy inland capital city. The man who designed it was Chicago architect Walter Burley Griffin, the winner of the world-wide National Capital Design Competition announced in 1911 and decided in 1912.

Canberra is on the news every night. This amazing phenomenon is simply because all the big boys who run Australia work and live here, as do all of the international ambassadors and their staff. About 70 per cent of the population work for the Government.

Canberra also has the National Art Gallery, National Library, National War Museum, Parliament House, lots of big buildings for Government research, big parks, wide

streets, lots of places to park, the best bike tracks in Australia, Questacon
(The National Science and Technology centre) and the High Court of Australia.

Redwood Memorial Grove

Located near Canberra Airport, this is worth a look. Thomas Weston, who was Walter Burley Griffin's horticulturalist, was very fond of redwoods and convinced Griffin to plant an immense forest of 120,000 trees. Due to many factors, including conditions not being suitable and the RAAF base being located close by, only 3,000 redwoods have survived – these are now listed in the Commonwealth Heritage List.

The Carillon

Twice a week, recitals of all kinds of music are played in this bell tower. Entering from a park on the edge of Lake Burley Griffin, you can catch the lift up to the top and listen to the bell music from about 20 m above Lake Burley Griffin.

Brindabella National Park

This alpine park runs along the western border of the Australian Capital Territory. This region has everything, and definite *Ooh Aah* qualities along with a bit of history; there are old alpine huts still standing and some arboreta – areas where trees were grown as test samples before they were grown in commercial plantations.

Although the tests were unsuccessful, their remnants have left bizarre groves of unusual trees amongst the eucalypt forest, from countries as varied as the Himalayas or South America.

Tidbinbilla Space Centre

This is one of only three deep space tracking centres in the world.

New South Wales

The Premier State

- •• **Area Covered:** 801,428 square km, or about
  10 per cent of Australia
- •• **Capital City:** Sydney
- •• **Longest River:** the Darling River
- •• **Highest Point:** Mount Kosciusko (2,229 m)
- •• **Highest Waterfall:** Wollomombi
- •• **Floral Emblem:** the Waratah
- •• **Faunal Emblems:** the Platypus and
  the Kookaburra
- •• **Motto:** Orta recens quam pura nites –
  "Newly risen, how bright you shine"

SOME STAR ATTRACTIONS OF NEW SOUTH WALES

Sydney

This is the largest city in Australia. Sydney's suburbs are
edged in the east with a coastline of surf beaches and
harbour bays. On the western side, they run towards the
Blue Mountains. Sydney Harbour is simply the most
breathtaking natural harbour in the world. One of the
best ways to view it is by riding on the Manly Ferry.

The Blue Mountains

Located inland from Sydney, this is a popular weekend
spot for Sydneysiders, with great views and exhausting
walking tracks (typical *Ooh Aah* experience). The Blue

NEW SOUTH WALES

Broken Hill

Lightning Ridge

Darling River

Walgett • Moree • Lismore • Cape Byron

Grafton

Cobar

Tamworth

Warrumbungle Range

Wilcannia

Wollomombi Falls ---- Highest waterfall. Port Macquarie

Dubbo

Orange

Hay

Bathurst

Blue Mountains

Lake George

SYDNEY

Riverina District
Wagga Wagga

Canberra

Albury

Snowy Mountains

ACT

Mount Kosciusko 2,229 m

Mountains appear as a hazy blue from a distance. It's thought the fumes from the eucalypt oils, mixed with the air and the light, create the blue colour.

Tamworth

This is the country music capital of Australia, which holds the Annual Country Music Festival and awards ceremonies each year.

The Snowy Mountains

As the name suggests, these are the snowfields of New South Wales. They are also the largest snowfields in Australia. The Snowy Mountains are popular with bush-walkers in summer.

Jenolan Caves

This is a network of caves and tunnels with wonderful limestone formations called stalactites and stalagmites.

The mites point up and the tites point down. These caves are great to walk through - it's like being on the set of "Dr Who"! The name Jenolan comes from the Aboriginal word Genowlan, meaning "high mountain".

Lake George
(Now you See it, Now you Don't)

The disappearing trick this 16 km wide lake seems to play intrigued people for many years. It may be full of water one month and a few months later may be almost empty, leaving sheep grazing on its grassy bed. This mystery has been solved - it turns out that the balance between the rain that falls and the moisture that evaporates is very finely tuned in this rather strange part of the world.

The Warrumbungle Range

This is full of walks, volcanic peaks and great views - another *Ooh Aah* experience.

Ophir

This minute town near Bathurst (so minute, it's not on our map) is the place where the first gold was discovered in Australia.

Lightning Ridge

This is home to the rare black opal, which has only ever been found in three other places on Earth.

Brookong Woolshed

This shed, found in the Riverina district, was once the largest in Australia. How large was it? Well, in 1886, 373,000 sheep were shorn here. Just read that again and think about it - amazing!

Victoria
The Garden State

- •• **Area covered:** about 228,000 sq km, or nearly 3 per cent of Australia
- •• **Capital City:** Melbourne
- •• **Longest River:** Goulburn River
- •• **Highest Point:** Mount Bogong (1,986 m)
- •• **Floral Emblem:** the Common Heath
- •• **Faunal Emblems:** Leadbeater's Possum and the Helmeted Honeyeater
- •• **Motto:** "Peace and prosperity"

THINGS TO SEE AND DO IN VICTORIA

Melbourne

The rival city to Sydney, Melbourne is famous for having the best restaurants and a great night life, and being the ultimate shopping stop. You can punt down the Yarra River from Fairfield Boathouse and follow this by a decadent afternoon tea, visit the Victorian Arts Centre, or walk through the Botanical Gardens.

Mount Bogong

This is the highest Victorian mountain, named after a moth. The word comes from the Aboriginal name for this insect, "bugong". You may see the moths when the wind blows them off course during their migration to the mountain areas of New South Wales and Victoria.

Gold Towns

Most of the gold that has been found in Australia came from the towns of Ballarat, Bendigo and Castlemaine.

Floating Islands Lagoon

Located south of Lake Corangamite, this lagoon has no fewer than four floating islands. The four unusual travellers are home to trees growing to 8 m in height. The islands have been known to float 100 m in an hour if there is a strong enough wind blowing.

The Murray River

If you visit historic Echuca you can relive Australia's past. Ride down the Murray River on the restored paddle boats, which were once used to take goods and passengers up and down the river. In the 1870s Echuca was the largest inland port in Australia.

The Twelve Apostles

Travelling along The Great Ocean Road, you will come across the Twelve Apostles, which are amazing huge columns of rock rising from the ocean.

The Grampians

Great walks, craggy peaks, stunning views; this is yet another *Ooh Aah* experience.

Wilsons Promontory

This offers you 80 km of *Ooh Aah* experiences, and great beaches.

Daring skier attempts to ride Mt Buffalo...

Mount Buffalo

One of three skiing regions in Australia.

SOUTH AUSTRALIA

Mount Woodroffe

Sturt National Park

Cooper Creek

Oodnadatta

Tirari Desert

Lake Eyre

Moomba

Coober Pedy

Sturt Desert

Marree

Great Victorian Desert

Lake Torrens

Flinders Ranges

Lake Frome

Nullarbor Plain

Penong

Ceduna

Lake Gairdner

Port Augusta

Port Pirie

Fowlers Bay

Whyalla

Murray River

Great Australian Bight

ADELAIDE

Eyre Peninsula

The Coolong

Port Lincoln

Kangaroo Island

Mt Gambier

South Australia

The Festival State

- **Area Covered:** 984,000 square km or about 13 per cent of Australia
- **Capital City:** Adelaide
- **Longest River:** Cooper Creek
- **Highest point:** Mount Woodroffe (1,439 m)
- **Floral Emblem:** Sturt's Desert Pea.
- **Faunal Emblem:** Hairy-nosed Wombat
- **Motto:** Ut prosint omnibus conjunti – "United for the common good"

INTEREST POINTS IN SOUTH AUSTRALIA

Adelaide

This lovely city is situated on Lake Torrens and is dominated by its architecture of early stone buildings, with the sea on one side and the Adelaide Hills on the other. It is most famous for the Adelaide Festival of the Arts, held every two years, and the Formula One Grand Prix, which bring a contrast to this normally calm and contented city.

Hahndorf

Originally settled by German families in 1839, this little town in the Adelaide hills has retained its 19th century German character. This town is so small that it's not on our map – but we assure you it's really there.

Mount Gambier

Vulcanologists, the scientists who study volcanoes, think that Australia's most recent eruption probably took place at Mount Gambier. The crater of the extinct volcano has four lakes in it. One of these, Blue Lake (also known as Devil's Inkbottle), changes colour in November each year, from grey to blue.

Koonalda Cave

Reputedly the oldest Aboriginal art in Australia has been scratched into the soft walls of Koonalda Cave, deep beneath the Nullarbor Plain. The artists, working about 20,000 years ago, used torches of burning wood to light the inky blackness of the cave.

Sturts Stony Desert

Only a hardy traveller should venture across Sturts Stony Desert. The stones after which it takes its name are so hard and sharp that Aboriginal people used them to make blades for their tools!

Lake Eyre

When it's full, this is the country's biggest lake. When it's empty (99.9 per cent of the time), it's a dry, flat salt pan.

The Coorong

This coastal lagoon, protected by sand dunes, stretches for 160 km. The landscape is wild and desolate and home

Surfie vulcanologist catches a hot lava wave!

to many sea birds and wildlife. It provided the setting for Colin Thiele's famous children's story "Stormboy".

Wilpena Pound

This is an amazing natural amphitheatre in the Flinders Ranges. The rocky walls of the amphitheatre encircle the central bowl for 35 km. There is only one tiny gap in the wall where you can get through into the bowl.

Western Australia

The State of Excitement

- •• **Area Covered:** 2,525,500 square km, or about 33 per cent of Australia
- •• **Capital City:** Perth
- •• **Longest River:** the Gascoyne River
- •• **Highest Point:** Mount Meharry (1,245 m)
- •• **Floral Emblem:** the Kangaroo Paw
- •• **Faunal Emblem:** the Numbat and the Black Swan
- •• **Motto:** none

WESTERN AUSTRALIAN HIGHLIGHTS

Perth

Built on the Swan River, a watersport paradise, Perth is quite sparse and clean-cut, with lots of parks and beaches. It's great to drive to Fremantle a few kilometres away, or picnic at Trigg Beach.

The Bungle Bungles

These are a remarkable collection of spires and domes of weathered rock scattered along a remote area in the far north of the state.

Monkey Mia

Nowhere in the world will you find friendlier bottle-nosed dolphins living in the wild than at Shark Bay,

850 km north of Perth. A group of these gentle creatures visit the beach at Monkey Mia regularly to be fed and patted by the 40,000 visitors who travel to this remote place each year just to see them.

The Royal Family

The 7,474 ha Principality of Hutt River Province was created by Leonard Casley in 1970. Prince Leonard, as he now calls himself, had a disagreement with the Commonwealth of Australia about the amount of wheat he was allowed to produce. This is why he took the unusual step of separating himself from the rest of the country. As many as 50,000 visitors make the 550 km journey from Perth each year to buy the local money, stamps and first-day covers, and to have their visas stamped.

Rottnest Island

This island is famous for its colony of quokkas, small, wallaby-like marsupials. It got its name when an early Dutch explorer saw a quokka from a distance and mistook it for a rat, "rott" in Dutch. The island is surrounded by reefs that make it excellent for diving.

Lake Argyle

This is the largest man-made lake in Western Australia. It was formed in 1971 by the damming of the Ord River as part of an irrigation project. The lake holds 5,672 million litres of water.

Modern day Quokka holidaying in Disneyland is mistaken for a rat yet again...

Hamersley Range National Park

This park boasts broad, steep-sided gorges that are another typical *Ooh Aah* experience.

The Canning Stock Route

In 1906 a 46-year-old surveyor, Alfred Canning, created a cattle track between Halls Creek in the Kimberley region and the start of the railway at Wiluna, 700 km from Perth. The 1,753 km Canning Stock Route is the most dangerous and difficult outback track ever to be blazed in Australia's history, as it crosses the dry and wild Tanami, Little Sandy and Great Sandy deserts. Once it had 51 waterholes available to thirsty travellers, but nowadays there are only 12. Anyone who wants an outback adventure following in the footsteps of the cattle that once trod the track should take a four-wheel-drive vehicle and plenty of water and fuel.

Mount Augustus

Have you ever heard of an upfaulted monoclinal gritty conglomerate? Well, Australia has one, called Mount Augustus. Located 320 km east of Carnarvon in Western Australia, it is twice the size of Uluru, measuring 8 km long by 3 km wide, and it is 377 m high.

Stirling Range

These mountains are well known for the beautiful wildflowers that bloom there each spring, and for which Western Australia is famous.

You can lead a horse to water, but it won't be able to pick up the glass...

Wave Rock

This is a natural rock structure that has been eroded and resembles a wave about to crash. It is much bigger than most visitors expect.

NORTHERN TERRITORY

Bathurst Island
Melville Island
Darwin
Kakadu National Park
Arnhem Land
Katherine Gorge
• Katherine
Gulf of Carpentaria
Groote Eylandt
'The Never-Never'
Victoria River
Barkly Tableland
Tanami Desert
• Tenant Creek
• Devil's Marbles
Mount Liebig 1,524m
Kata Tjuta
Alice Springs
Lake Neale
Amadeus
Lake
Henbury Station
Finke River
Simpson Desert
Todd River
Ayers Rock/Uluru
Uluru National Park

Northern Territory

Outback Australia

- •• **Area Covered:** 1,346,200 square km, or about 15.5 per cent of Australia
- •• **Capital City:** Darwin
- •• **Longest River:** the Victoria River
- •• **Highest Point:** Mount Liebig (1,524 m)
- •• **Floral Emblem:** Sturt's Desert Rose
- •• **Faunal Emblems:** the Red Kangaroo and the Wedge-tailed Eagle
- •• **Motto:** none

OTHER THINGS ABOUT THE NORTHERN TERRITORY

Darwin

This is the city of the outback, beaches, heat and crocodiles, famous for the day Cyclone Tracy destroyed the city and everyone's Christmas celebrations. Many say the rebuilding of Darwin after the cyclone rebuilt the people's spirit, and as a result it is a better place to live.

Henbury Cattle Station

If you visit Henbury cattle station near Alice Springs, you'll see 13 craters formed when a meteorite fell to Earth. The largest is 15 m deep and measures 220 m by 110 m. The meteorite landed about 4,700 years ago, and must have been seen by the local Aboriginal people, whose name for the area means "Sun walk fire devil rock". It is estimated that 130 meteorites have fallen on Australia.

▲

Uluru

Formerly called Ayers Rock, this is the largest monolith in the world, and the heart of Australia's red centre. This extraordinary formation attracts tens of thousands of visitors each year.

Katherine

This area is famous for its gorge. Divided into 13 canyons, the gorge has spectacular 70 m high walls that change colour with the light.

Kata Tjuta

These great rocks, formerly called the Olgas, are a group of monoliths many people find even grander than Uluru.

Devil's Marbles

The Aboriginal people believe that the Devil's Marbles, north of Alice Springs, are eggs laid by a giant serpent. A more mundane explanation is that they are large pieces of granite that have eroded far more slowly than the soil around them, leaving them piled up precariously on top of one another.

Kakadu National Park

The showplace of the Northern Territory, Kakadu National Park, east of Darwin, is home to hundreds of species of birds and animals (including freshwater crocodiles), and preserves an incredible number of Aboriginal rock paintings. More than 300 galleries have

Crocodile snaps at a skinny-dipping tourist!

been found by Europeans, but it is estimated that there are a further 1,000 or so known only to the Aboriginal people.

Queensland

The Sunshine State

- •• **Area Covered:** 1,727,200 square km or about 23 per cent of Australia
- •• **Capital City:** Brisbane
- •• **Longest River:** the Flinders River
- •• **Highest Point:** Mount Bartle Frere (1,612 m)
- •• **Floral Emblem:** the Cooktown Orchid
- •• **Faunal Emblems:** the Koala and the Brolga
- •• **Motto:** Audux at fidelis – 'Bold – yes, and faithful too!'

A SELECTION OF QUEENSLAND INTEREST POINTS

Brisbane

Brisbane, like all of Queensland, has a distinctive character. This is mainly due to the "Queenslanders", the typical weatherboard homes on stilts, often with verandahs and fretwork. These houses were designed for maximum airflow and coolness through the hot summers.

The Brisbane River winds through the city, which has great coffee shops, clubs and art galleries. And, of course, the Gold Coast is only an hour's drive away.

Surfers Paradise

The most famous beach on the Gold Coast, this is one of Australia's favourite playgrounds. Its long white beaches and many shopping areas, theme parks and

Torres Strait

Great Barrier Reef

Weipa

Gulf of Carpentaria

Daintree River

Daintree National Park

Wellesley Isls

Normanton

Cairns

1612m

Burketown

Mount Bartle Frere

Flinders River

Townsville

Whitsunday Islands

Mount Isa

Charters Towers

Mackay

Burke.

Longreach

Rockhampton

Emerald

Fraser Island

Birdsville

Great Dividing Range

Marlborough

Glasshouse Mountains

Quilpie

Charleville

Nambour

Brisbane

Cunnamulla

Surfers Paradise

QUEENSLAND

How Rainforests get their name...

restaurants mean that many Australians choose to holiday here.

The Daintree River

This area of dense tropical rainforest meets the idyllic waters of the reef – a paradise!

Fraser Island

Also known as the Great Sandy Island, this is the biggest sand island in the world. It is 120 km long, varies from 4 to 22 km wide and is 240 m high at its tallest point. Surprisingly, this sandy island contains over 40 freshwater lakes and an ancient belt of rainforest down its middle.

The Glasshouse Mountains

Here the polished rock of the 11 peaks reflects sunlight and shines like glass.

Morning Glory

Visit Burke Town between August and November and you may see one of the most amazing formations of cloud in the world. The roll of cloud, often 700 km long and 1 km wide, will suddenly appear on the horizon just after sunrise, hence its nickname, "Morning Glory".

The Great Barrier Reef

This is the largest and most spectacular reef in the world. To visit the reef you can stay on one of the many islands that dot its length. If you are leaving from the mainland, Cairns is one of the most popular departure points.

Australian Stockmans Hall of Fame

This is a great museum, dedicated to the history of the Australian outback. It is situated at Longreach.

Tasmania
The Holiday Isle

- •• **Area Covered:** 68,331 square km, or nearly 1 per cent of Australia
- •• **Capital City:** Hobart
- •• **Longest River:** the South Esk River
- •• **Highest Point:** Mount Ossa (1,617 m)
- •• **Floral Emblem:** the Tasmanian Blue Gum
- •• **Faunal Emblem:** the Tasmanian Devil
- •• **Motto:** Ubertas et fidelitas - "Fertility and faithfulness"

GREAT THINGS IN TASSY

Hobart

The city of Hobart is the smallest and the second oldest capital city. It is also home to Australia's oldest museum and oldest tennis court, say no more! But seriously, built on the mouth of the Derwent River, Hobart is an enjoyable city with mountains rising behind it.

Mount Wellington

Towering above Hobart, Mount Wellington provides visitors with great views of the city and out to sea.

Port Arthur

This is a convict settlement with a very black history. Between 1830 and 1850, about 12,500 convicts passed through its cells. About 1,800 convicts lie buried on the

Serious bushwalker arrives at the best view yet on his marathon hike through the wilderness...

Isle of the Dead across the bay. It is not surprising that this eerie place is supposed to be haunted by unhappy ghosts!

Cradle Mountain National Park

Serious bushwalkers fly in from all over the world to go walking in this famous park. The 85 km, five-day trek skirts the 17 km long Lake St Clair (Australia's deepest lake). Forest-filled valleys and mountain ridges afford spectacular views, *Ooh Aah!*

The Gordon River

This is one of the wildest and most beautiful rivers in Australia. A boat journey along its length takes you between steep black walls of rock and over racing rapids.

The Southernmost Manned Lighthouse in Australia

The lighthouse stands on one of the Maatsuyker Islands, about 10 km from the Tasmanian mainland. Until 1928, homing pigeons carried messages between the remote islands and the lighthouse headquarters, which were located in Hobart.

Ben Lomond

This volcanic plateau is Tasmania's most popular skiing resort in winter.

Our Beloved Beach

Ho hum, another day in paradise!

Australia has some of the most beautiful and isolated beaches in the world, running along the majority of our coastline. Understandably, the beach is a big part of the Australian way of life.

Tips for Safe Beach Swimming

- Swim on patrolled beaches between the red and yellow flags.
- Don't swim immediately after eating.
- Always pick a point on the beach as your reference, and look at it after each wave, making sure you are still in line. This way you won't accidentally drift too far.

Slip, Slop, Slap

If you were born or spent your childhood in Australia, you are automatically in the high risk category for skin cancer.

Gory Skin Cancer Facts

- The main cause of skin cancer is too much sun.
- Skin cancer is the most common cancer in Australia.

- •• Australians have the highest rate of skin cancer in the world.
- •• About 1,000 people die each year in Australia from skin cancer.
- •• Every year there are about 140,000 new cases.
- •• Most skin cancers can be prevented by protecting yourself from the sun.
- •• Skin cancer can be cured if detected and treated early.

Be Sensible Little Vegemites

- •• Slap on a hat with a broad brim.
- •• Slop on a good sunscreen with a protection factor of 15+.
- •• Slip on a shirt.

Bluebottles

Bluebottles are a well-known pest on our beaches in summer. They occur in large groups in the open oceans and are washed up on the beaches by onshore winds. If you see them on the sand, they will be in the water too. They look like a blue bubble of gum with a long blue tentacle trailing behind. If the tentacles stick to your skin, their stinging cells can cause an excruciating pain that takes hours to ease. If you swim amongst them, it is easy to get stung, but even if they are washed up on the beach they will still be active. A favourite Aussie pastime is popping the bluebottles on the beach (if you try it, make sure you wear shoes. As responsible publishers, we have to make sure we don't encourage reckless behaviour. Therefore any bluebottle bashing is entirely at your own risk.)

First Aid for Bluebottle Stings

••• Carefully remove the bluebottle from your skin, so as not to get stung again.

••• Rub the stung area with wet sand.

••• If there are lifesavers nearby, run to them screaming; they will usually have something on hand to alleviate the pain.

••• If no one is on hand to help, go to a chemist or try vinegar.

Hungry bluebottle comes in out of the surf after a long swim for a bite to eat...

jeremy

(Jaws Music)

Since 1900, about 420 people have been killed in
Australia by sharks. Here are some typical hints that are
passed down through Australian families on how to cut
down your chances of being attacked.

Shark with a highly
evolved dorsal fin
that acted as a
deadly lifesaver lure...

Uncle Kevin's Code of Shark-safe Beach Behaviour

••• Don't go out ridiculously far.

••• Don't swim at dawn or dusk or in the dark.

••• If it looks like sharkie weather, it probably is.

••• Stick to patrolled beaches.

••• Dogs attract sharks. Don't swim with your dog on an unpatrolled beach.

••• Don't swim with seals, for the same reason.

••• Avoid swimming in quiet bays and inland waterways that lead to the sea, as these are common shark breeding grounds.

••• Use your common sense and trust your feelings.

Don't Get Carried Away!

Get a group of Australians together in a room, and they will all have a story about THE TIME THEY GOT CAUGHT IN A RIP.

Mr Macquarie's definition of a rip is:

"**1.** a disturbance in the sea caused by opposing currents or by a fast current passing over an uneven bottom. **2.** a fast current, esp. one at a beach which can take swimmers out to sea. **3.** to cut or tear away in a rough or vigorous manner."

These definitions won't help you if you ever get caught in a rip, so we ditched the reference books and went to the lifesavers for advice.

Somebody's Uncle who was Once a Lifesaver's Rip Survival Techniques

How to spot a rip:
Sometimes you can tell if there is a rip. The foam from the waves breaking is going over the back of the waves and out to sea even though the waves are pulling the water forward.

What to do if you didn't read the first paragraph:
If you get caught, do not panic.

Do not try to swim against the current. Swim diagonally across it. If you get too tired, float on your back and raise your hand. If no one sees you go out with the rip, swim around it and come back in at a different point. A rip will always weaken.

Lifesaver, Ninety Mile Beach...

Lifesaving

The famous image of the bronzed Aussie comes from our surf lifesavers. Besides protecting us at our beaches, they take part in a variety of beach competitions, the most popular being the Iron Man. The Iron Man competition tests the many skills of a surf lifesaver. Competitors in this endurance race must be able to swim, paddle a rescue board and a surf ski and then sprint along the sand to the finish line.

Since the Surf Life Saving Association with its distinctive red and yellow caps was formed in 1907, 344,000 swimmers have been rescued from danger in Australian seas. The first rescue took place at Bondi Beach. Two boys were rescued using the reel and rope method. One of these boys was Charles Kingsford Smith, who, thanks to the Surf Life Saving Association, would later go on to become Australia's most famous aviator.

▲

Brilliant Australian Swimmer, laden with a swag of Gold medals, unavoidably begins training as a weight-lifter for the next Olympics...

Jeremy

Our Sporting Life

We are a nation of sportsmen and sportswomen. If we don't play sport, we follow it. Our mild climate means outdoor sports are possible all year round and our long summers mean watersports are a favourite.

Swimming

Australians are famous for swimming. In fact, Australian Richard Cavill invented the "Australian Crawl" in 1899, now known as freestyle.

Golden Swimmers

Australian swimming has produced more international champions and collected more Olympic Gold Medals than any other sport in this country.

Our Hero

Dawn Fraser set more world records than any other Australian swimmer, with her amazing 27 individual and 12 relay world records.

Surfing

Surfing, like swimming, plays a part in many Australians' lives. Australians are always present in the elite group of world champion surfers. Mark Richards took out the World Surfing Championships four years in a row from 1979 to 1982. This record has not yet been broken.

Sailing

Australia's most famous yacht race is the Sydney to Hobart Yacht Race. The competitors leave from Sydney every Boxing Day and sail 1,167 km to Hobart. It takes them about two and a half to four days to get there.

The Race that Stopped the Nation

One of our most famous sailing achievements was in 1983, when "Australia II", with its controversial "winged keel", designed by Ben Lexen, won the Americas Cup at Newport, Rhode Island in the USA. Every Australian remembers the day when we ended 112 years of American domination of the race.

Single-handed Champion

Kay Cottee became the first woman to sail around the world single-handedly when she sailed into Sydney Harbour on 5 June 1988. This adventurous Australian yachtswoman travelled 46,000 km and spent over five months aboard her yacht "Blackmore's First Lady".

Yuppie Surfer with
a mobile wave...

Fishing

This is an absolute favourite of the masses. It is estimated that 1.75 million people go fishing at least once every year. The majority fish for pleasure rather than competition. Australia has great fishing grounds, and keen fishermen and fisherwomen and fisherkids travel from all over the world to fish here.

Cricket

As soon as summer hits it is cricket season in Australia. Our most famous cricketing legend is Donald Bradman, who played cricket between 1927 and 1948. His highest score – 452 runs against Queensland in 1928 – remains a record. He still holds the record for the highest score in Australian test match history – 334 runs. Allan Border, who started playing test matches in 1976 and is currently Captain of the Australian team, will also go down in history as one of our greats.

Australia has beaten every other country's test team more times than they have beaten Australia.

Football

There are four types of football played in Australia. The most popular are the rival codes of Aussie Rules and League. Football is considered a winter sport.

Aussie Rules

Australian Rules was invented in Australia. There are 18 people on each team. The players leap in the air a lot and wear sleeveless shirts. This is the most popular type of football in Tasmania, Victoria, Western Australia and South Australia. Roy Cazaly was a famous Tasmanian Aussie Rules player who was able to leap an incredible 1.5 m from the ground to catch the ball.

The most people ever to watch a sporting event at a sports ground in Australia's history gathered in 1970: nearly 122,000 people squashed into the Melbourne Cricket Ground to watch the VFL Australian Rules grand final – Carlton versus Collingwood.

Rugby League

Rugby League has 13 players on each side and is the favourite in New South Wales and Queensland. Players must run with the ball to score a try and to earn the right to kick for goal. These footballers tend to wear traditional long-sleeved football jerseys.

The hero Herbert Henry "Dally" Messenger once kicked an 82 m goal from Australia's 25 yard line against England – a kick that has never been beaten.

Freak Rugby League Injury

Rugby Union

Rugby Union is keenly followed in Queensland and New South Wales and this form of football is played with 15 players on each side.

Faster than Rugby League, Union is popular, and played in national and international competitions. The Australian Union team are called the "Wallabies", one of the top teams in the world. The catch-cry, "Waddaya-wanna-be? A walla-walla-by!" is shouted out by fans wherever the team goes.

The stars of Australian Rugby Union are David Campese and Michael Lynagh. David holds the world record for the most tries scored in a career (37 tries in 52 games), while Michael holds the record for the most points (564 points from 43 games).

Soccer

Soccer is played everywhere except Western Australia and the Northern Territory. There are 11 players on each side. This game is most popular with young players under 12 as an introduction to team ball play, and is considered safer physically than any other code of football. The Australian soccer teams are starting to develop a respected place in international competition.

Tennis

Australians have had more champion players in tennis than in any other sport except swimming. Evonne Goolagong, Ken Rosewall, John Newcombe, Margaret

Court and Rod Laver, the "Rocket", are some of the past greats. Rod Laver is the only person to have won the Grand Slam twice – in 1962 and 1969. He was also the first man to become a millionaire from tennis, a status he achieved in 1972.

John Newcombe has the record for men's wins at Wimbledon. He has won nine times (three men's singles titles and six men's doubles).

Netball

Netball is the most popular women's sport in Australia. There are over 750,000 registered players.

Basketball

Basketball's popularity in Australia has skyrocketed. Ten years ago, the average attendance at national games was 300. Today the average is 10,000.

Basketball is a popular team sport for both males and females. It has quite a cult following, featuring in many music videos, and influencing fashion and even slang – yo!

Mountain Climbing

Australia has produced a great number of adventurers and explorers of the peaks. Australian mountaineer Tim McCartney-Snape is the first person in the world to have travelled by foot from sea level to the highest point on Earth – the 8,848 m summit of Mount Everest.

Skiing – Australian Style

Compared to the rest of the world, our ski season is short, and even our longest runs are a hiccup compared to the Swiss Alps. Though we have had some winter sport champions, the majority of the Australian population tend to ski more in a thrash-and-burn style, as few of us had months of training as children to perfect our style.

Motor Sports

Australians love a petrol head.

The Australian Formula One Grand Prix

On a par with Monaco, Adelaide hosts this major
international motor-racing event. For the week leading
up to the big race, friendly, quiet Adelaide is
transformed. Our most famous Grand Prix racer is Sir
Jack Brabham. Alan Jones won three Grand Prix races
in a row, and once won four Grand Prix races in one
season, in 1978.

The Bathurst 1000

This is Australia's most famous and popular touring car
championship, broadcast to millions around the world.
Some of our champions include the well-known Peter
Brock, Bob Jane and Allan Moffatt.

Motor Bikes

Motor bikes have always been popular in Australia. Our
climate means riding is possible all year round, and
races are cheaper and easier to organise than the car
races.

Wayne Gardner is definitely one of our all-time-
great sporting heroes. His win of the World Motorcycling
Grand Prix 500cc class in 1987 made the already keenly
followed sport enormously popular in Australia.

After speedway racing, motorcycle racing is the
biggest killer of all Australian sports.

PETROL HEAD...

Australian Boxing's secret weapon...

Boxing

I feel no pain!

Australia has had and still has great boxing champions. Jeff Fenech is the only Australian to win three world titles. Lionel Rose was one of the first Aboriginal sports competitors to win international status, when he won the World Bantam-weight title at 19. Tony Mundine never lost a fight to another Australian, scored more knock-out victories than any other Australian and won world ranking in three divisions.

Golf

Great climate, great golf! There are approximately 1,400 golf clubs in Australia, with one million players. The Australian Open is an international golfing tournament. One of our greatest is Greg Norman, "The Great White Shark", whose earnings are thought to be approximately $10 million a year.

Athletics

Australia has had many athletics champions, from marathon runners like Robert de Castella, Herb Elliot (the 1500 m king), Betty Cuthbert (the Golden Girl winner of four Olympic golds) and Ron Clarke - 17 world records have been set by our champions. Most of us humble folk, if involved in athletics, only ever enjoyed Little Athletics for kids on a Saturday.

Biggest Event

With more than 30,000 competitors each year, the City to Surf, held every August, is the country's largest sporting event. The race starts from Sydney's Hyde Park and finishes in the surfside suburb of Bondi 14 km away.

The race record was set by Steve Moneghetti in 1991 when he ran the distance in 40 minutes and three seconds. He has also set a further record by winning the race four times in a row. The best women's time was achieved by Lisa Martin in 1988, when she ran 45 minutes and 47 seconds.

Horse Racing

Australians love a bet, and horse racing is no exception. It is keenly followed all year.

The Race of Champions

At 3.00 pm on the first Tuesday of every November, the nation holds its breath for the running of the Melbourne Cup, Australia's richest and most famous horse race. The whole nation loves this day – women everywhere wear hats, every office holds a betting sweep, people drag their televisions into work and everybody looks forward to a big lunch. And all of this in expectation of a three-minute race.

Melbourne Cup Day in Victoria is a public holiday, and by the look of it nearly the whole population of Melbourne attends the race.

Divided Loyalties

Phar Lap, the most famous horse in racing history and a Melbourne Cup winner, has had his remains spread over three different museums. His heart is in the National Museum, his stuffed skin is in the State Museum of Victoria, and his skeleton is in the National Museum of New Zealand, in Wellington!

The Great Phar Lap winning by a nose...

I can throw your gumboot further than anyone else in the world!
You're pulling my leg!

Serious Sports

Throwing – Australian Style

Eggs

Mike Skinner threw a fresh hen's egg 87.7 m in 1985. Luckily, it was caught by a Mr T. Bennet. The event took place at the Adelaide Grand Prix.

Spears

In 1982 Bailey Bush threw a spear with the aid of a woomera a mighty 99.51 m in Camden, New South Wales.

Gumboots

The Australian record for gumboot throwing was set by Roland Doom when he tossed a boot 44.2 m at the agricultural show in Victoria in 1978.

Darwin Aluminium Can Regatta

This is a boat race with a difference. Thousands of empty cans are used to build a variety of seagoing craft, from simple skiffs to model galleons.

Henley-on-Todd Regatta

Australia's strangest boat race, the Henley-on-Todd Regatta, is held along the dry bed of the Todd River. The novelty races include propelling boats along the river on metal tracks while others carry their boats and stage 'sea battles' using flour-bombs as ammunition.

Yarra Dragon Boat Races

A spectacular carnival is held each year on the Yarra River in Melbourne. The colourful Dragon Boats need a large, very disciplined team to propel them efficiently through the water. In each boat a drum is beaten so the many oarsmen can keep in time.

The Great Sydney Harbour Ferry Boat Race

The annual race of Sydney Harbour's passenger ferries is the highlight of the Sydney Festival in January. The whole harbour comes alive with spectator boats, as people watch their favourite ferry compete.

Good Aussie Tucker– Australian Food

Our cuisine is rich and varied. With the most amazing choice of seafoods, meats, fruit and vegetables available all year round, a great climate for outdoor eating, and a world-wide range of cultural influences, Australian cuisine is acquiring its own character.

Les tackles a bowl of spag bol...

Say What?

These are some of our favourite food terms:

- ••• **grub** - food
- ••• **barbie** - barbecue
- ••• **chew-'n'-spew** - typical take-away-type fried foods such as chips and hamburgers
- ••• **little lunch, play lunch** - morning tea at school
- ••• **brekkie** - breakfast
- ••• **big lunch** - lunch at school
- ••• **counter lunch** - lunch served at the pub
- ••• **din-din** - evening meal or dinner
- ••• **din-dins** - have a guess
- ••• **dinnies**- you guessed it
- ••• **tea** - tricked you, this can also mean dinner as well as a-cuppa-tea
- ••• **sweets** - dessert
- ••• **snag** - sausage
- ••• **chook** - chicken
- ••• **vegies** - vegetables
- ••• **goog or googy-egg** - runny egg
- ••• **spag bol** - spaghetti bolognaise
- ••• **bickie** - biscuit
- ••• **sanger or sambo** - sandwich
- ••• **the munchies** - an irresistible urge to eat

Don't Try to Shop only Once a Year!

If all the food bought each year in Australia was divided equally by our population, this would mean each person eats on average, in a year:

- 128 eggs
- 101 litres of milk
- 434 potatoes
- 66 loaves of bread
- 165 oranges
- 72 bananas
- 21,552 peas
- 6,622 teaspoons of sugar
- 63 kilos of red meat
- 40 chickens
- 2 kilos of coffee
- 1 kilo of tea

All-time Favourites

Besides "barbies", there are also a few traditional favourites we'll always call our own. Vegemite, meat pies, damper, lamingtons and pavlovas – what a mix!

A Happy Little Vegemite

Many Australians can recite the jingle for the Vegemite and the Aeroplane Jelly ads – what a nation!

Vegemite was invented in 1923, the same year they started building the Sydney Harbour Bridge. Fred Walker

Novice chef accidentally throws another snag on Barbie...

of Melbourne whipped up the first batch – no, not from axle grease, he used the scum from the brewer's yeast at the Carlton United Breweries – gross!

Vegemite is rich in vitamin B, so the ad tells us, and is usually served on toast at breakfast or in bed with a cuppa tea by mum when you're feeling sick. It's also a favourite for school sandwiches, because it's easier to make than salad sandwiches. The trick for any foreigners willing to try it is to use a smudge, not a slab.

Though it originated here, we're afraid Vegemite is not Australian-owned.

Meat Pies

A favourite at school canteens and for lunch on the run. An old-fashioned variation on the meat pie 'n' sauce is pie 'n' peas, which is mushy pea slop, either in the pie or for the pie to sit in. What's in a meat pie? If any of our readers can tell us, please write in.

The Bread of the Outback

Damper is the traditional bread of the Australian stockman, cooked in the ashes of an open fire. The hard crust encases a soft, scone-like filling. In the country, damper is often served up with "Cocky's Joy" Golden Syrup and lashes of butter. The biggest damper that was ever made measured 21.52 m long and 2.32 m wide. It weighed 9 kg and was baked at the Buttercup Bakery in North Ryde, New South Wales.

Here is a typical damper recipe taken from *The Macquarie Dictionary of Cookery:*

Ingredients
3 cups self-raising flour
1 1/2 teaspoons salt
90 g butter
1/2 cup milk
1/2 cup water
extra flour

Method
Sift the flour and salt into a bowl, and then rub in the butter until the mixture resembles fine breadcrumbs. Make a well in the centre of the dry ingredients and add the combined milk and water, all at once, mixing lightly with a knife in a cutting motion. Turn out onto a lightly floured surface and knead gently. Work the dough into a round shape approximately 15 cm in diameter. With a sharp knife, cut a cross in the surface of the dough 1 cm deep. Brush the surface of the dough with milk and dust lightly with extra flour. Bake in a hot oven for 10 minutes and then reduce the heat to 180°C and bake for a further 15 minutes or until golden brown.

Stale Cake for the Governor

The lamington, sponge cake covered with chocolate and coconut, is said to have been invented by a grazier's wife in Queensland around the turn of the century. She covered some cake in chocolate and coconut to prevent it from getting stale and served it up to her husband's shearers as Lamington Cake in honour of the current Queensland governor, Charles Wallace Ballie, the Baron Lamington!

The largest lamington that has ever been made was prepared by the staff of the Inter-Continental Hotel in Sydney as part of the hotel's fifth birthday celebrations. It weighed a mighty 452 kg and used 1,500 eggs.

NB. Lemmings are mouse-like critters from Scandinavia famous for their methods of population control - jumping off cliffs on mass.

To make a normal-size batch of lamingtons, follow this recipe from *The Macquarie Dictionary of Cookery:*

Ingredients
125 g butter or margarine
3/4 cup castor sugar
2 eggs
3 cups self-raising flour
1/2 cup milk
1/2 teaspoon vanilla

Icing
3 to 4 tablespoons boiling water
30 g butter
2 tablespoons cocoa
2 cups icing sugar, sifted
2 cups desiccated coconut

Method
Cream the butter and sugar until light and fluffy. Add in eggs one at a time, beating well between each addition. Fold in sifted flour alternately with combined milk and vanilla. Pour mixture into a greased lamington tin. Bake at 180°C for 30 to 40 minutes. Turn onto a cake rack to cool. Make the cake a day or two before cutting and icing the lamingtons, as fresh cake will usually crumble. Cut the cake into 5 cm squares.

To make the icing, pour boiling water over butter, add cocoa and mix well. Beat in the icing sugar until the mixture is smooth. Using a long-pronged fork, dip each piece of cake into the chocolate icing and roll in coconut. Then leave the squares to set on a cake rack.

To add some entertainment, cover a few squares of car sponge with chocolate and coconut to serve along with the real lamingtons. If you choose the rubber sponge well, this will work perfectly.

▲

A Dancer's Dessert

One of Australia's favourite desserts, the pavlova was created by Perth chef Bert Sachse in 1935. He named his creation after the famous Russian ballerina Anna Pavlova, who was visiting Australia at the time. Lighter than air, the meringue case of this classic dessert does resemble the frills of a ballerina's tutu.

To make your own pavlova you should follow this recipe from *The Macquarie Dictionary of Cookery:*

Ingredients
4 egg whites
$^1/_2$ teaspoon salt
1 $^1/_2$ teaspoons castor sugar
$^1/_2$ teaspoon vanilla
1 teaspoon vinegar
1 tablespoon cornflour
1 $^1/_4$ cups (300ml) pure cream, whipped
strawberries
kiwi fruit, peeled and sliced
passionfruit pulp
sliced banana, or any other soft fruit

Method
Place egg whites and salt in a large, clean, dry bowl and beat until soft peaks form. Gradually add the sugar, a tablespoon at a time, beating well after each addition. Lightly fold in the vinegar, vanilla and cornflour. Turn out onto a prepared (greased and floured) round plate and mould the mixture into a large round shape (approximately 40 cm in diameter) with an indentation in the centre. Bake at 120°C for 1 $^1/_2$ hours or until firm to the touch. When cool, place on a serving plate, fill with whipped cream and decorate with the fruit.

The Australian Language... da ta da ... brought to you by the Macquarie Dictionary Boffins

Australian English

The Macquarie Dictionary is Australia's national dictionary. It was written by Australians for Australians, using the Australian way of pronouncing and using words. Australian English has some unique words and phrases that you may use yourself or have heard other people using.

Australian English began with the arrival of the First Fleet at Botany Bay. In this strange wild country, there were many odd creatures, trees and flowers to be named. The new settlers borrowed some of the words they needed from the Aboriginal people they listened to. Examples of these borrowed words are billabong, dingo, galah, koala, kookaburra, kurrajong, mulga and waratah.

Slang

Slang words have always been popular in Australian English. Have you heard any of these?

- **Galah** or **ning nong** for a silly person.
- **Rubbity-dub** for a pub.
- **Bananabender** for a Queenslander.
- **Cornstalk** for a New South Welshman.
- **Cabbage-gardener** or **gumsucker** for a Victorian.
- **Apple Islander** or **Tassie** for a Tasmanian.
- **Top-ender** for a Territorian.
- **(Sand)groper** or **Westralian** for a Western Australian.
- **Croweater** or **wheatlander** for a South Australian.

We use slang for the jobs people do as well. Here are some of them.

- **Beak** for a judge or a schoolmaster.
- **Boss cocky** for a farmer who has people working for him.
- **Brickie** for a bricklayer.
- **Cop** for a police officer.
- **Crim** for a criminal.
- **Doc** for a doctor.
- **Journo** for a journalist.
- **Milko** for a milkman.
- **Muso** for a musician.
- **Ringer** for a station hand.

▲
phew, page **144**

- **Salt** for a sailor, especially an experienced one.
- **Schoolie** for a schoolteacher.
- **Schoolkid** for a school-aged child.
- **Swaggie** for a swagman.

Rebel mossie lives life on the edge...

sniff!

Short Words

Aussies like making words shorter too. Do you use any of these?

- I'll come over this **arvo** (afternoon).
- Throw the snags on the **barbie** (barbecue).
- Grab another **bickie** (biscuit) from the tin.
- Ow! The **mossies** (mosquitoes) are biting tonight.
- Our great land of **Oz** (Australia).
- Look out! **Roos** (kangaroos) cross here.

Strine

Before long, Australians started to sound different from people in other English-speaking countries. We sometimes call our Australian way of speaking Strine. Here are some funny re-spellings of what some of us say, collected by Professor Afferbeck Lauder in his book *Let Stalk Strine.* The Professor's real name is Alastair Morrison and, in case you hadn't realised, "Afferback Lauder" is Strine for "alphabetical order":

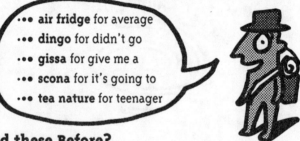

- **air fridge** for average
- **dingo** for didn't go
- **gissa** for give me a
- **scona** for it's going to
- **tea nature** for teenager

Heard these Before?

Here are some more Aussie words or sayings.

Do you **bludge** through school? If you do, then you refuse to take responsibility for anything: you don't work, you don't play, you don't join clubs, you just do nothing at all.

If you say that you're completely **bushed**, you mean that you're absolutely exhausted.

If someone calls you a real **dag**, they aren't giving you a compliment. In fact they think you lack style and that you're far too nerdy and conservative to be seen with. You'll probably find that they avoid you until you **get with it** or become cool.

To **come the raw prawn** on or with someone is to try to deceive them or to pretend that something is much better than it really is. Most people use it with "not", as in "Don't come the raw prawn with me."

Funnily enough, **to cop it** is to be punished for something but **to cop it sweet** is to have a lucky break. Then again, if your friends shout **cop this!**, they want you to look at something, usually so that you can admire it.

G'day is short for "May you have a good day " and is a friendly way of saying "how are you going" or "hi!" to someone. You can safely use this greeting whenever you want, not just in the daytime.

If you're **mates** with someone, then you're good friends with them, but people sometimes say **How are you going, mate?** to others just to be friendly and not because they're best buddies.

Have you ever wondered what **Matilda** is in Waltzing Matilda? Well, it's the "swag", or rolled up bundle of belongings, carried by someone travelling in the bush. To waltz Matilda is, simply, to carry your swag or travel the road.

You say **no worries** when you're absolutely sure that everything is going to be okay or if something isn't going to cause any trouble.

You should hang on to a dog or mate you think is **true blue** because you'll find that they're faithful, loyal and above board.

You beaut! is a good thing to say when you're really pleased or enthusiastic about something.

▲

A hot new television station comes to the bush...
Marg! They've got a log fire on tonight!

Extra Interesting and Useless Information to Fill up the Back of the Book

Note: all of these very interesting figures are approximations.

- •• **Births** – there are 245,000 babies born every year
- •• **Deaths** – there are 120,000 deaths every year
- •• **Male to female ratio** – there are 99.7 males to every 100 females in Australia
- •• **Number of primary school students** – 1,351, 665 students at public schools, 452,705 students at private schools
- •• **Number of secondary school students** – 882,418 public school students, 412,178 primary school students
- •• **School of the Air** – this transmits lessons from 12 cities to children in the remote outback
- •• **National Parks** – there are 515 National Parks in Australia
- •• **Hearing aids** – 108,000 hearing aids are supplied to Australians every year
- •• **TVs** – there were 6,500,000 television sets in Australia as at ten years ago (this means 99 per cent of Australian households have TVs)
- •• **Television stations** – there are 50 across Australia
- •• **Video machines** – 60 per cent of Australian households own a video player
- •• **Radios** – there are 20,000,000 radios in this country
- •• **Butcher shops** – 5,088 in Australia

- •• **Telephones** – there are 7,786,000 phones, and they make 10,695 million calls a year
- •• **Movie attendance** – Australians go to the movies 30.5 million times every year
- •• **Pets** – one in five Australians owns a dog, one in seven a cat
- •• **Lavish Gifts** – the publisher's birthday is on 3 November
- •• **Mail** – Australia Post processes about 4,119 million articles of mail per year and delivers to about 7 million addresses.
- •• **Cars** – there were 6,985,400 passenger cars by 1986
- •• **Roads** – there are 810,000 km of roads for all these cars to drive on

Australia's Time Zones

There are three time zones in Australia:

- •• **zone 1.** Western Australia
- •• **zone 2.** Northern Territory and South Australia
- •• **zone 3.** Tasmania, Victoria, New South Wales and Queensland

If it is 10 am in **zone 1**, it is 11.30 am in **zone 2** and 12 noon in **zone 3**.

This of course goes a bit haywire in summer when daylight saving is implemented. The clocks are all put forward by one hour except in Queensland and Western Australia.

Distances by Road

The distances in the table below are in kilometres.

Here are the codes for the table.

1 = Adelaide

2 = Brisbane

3 = Canberra

4 = Darwin

5 = Melbourne

6 = Perth

7 = Sydney

	1	2	3	4	5	6	7
Adelaide		2130	1210	3215	745	2750	1430
Alice Springs	1690	3060	2755	1525	2435	3770	2930
Brisbane	2130		1295	3495	1735	4390	1030
Broome	4035	4320	5100	1965	4780	2415	4885
Cairns	2865	1840	3140	2795	3235	6015	2870
Canberra	1210	1295		4230	655	3815	305
Darwin	3215	3495	4230		3960	4345	4060
Melbourne	755	1735	655	3960		3495	895
Perth	2750	4390	3815	4345	3495		3990
Sydney	1430	1030	305	4060	895	3990	

If any of our readers have any other useless, useful, or interesting facts please write and tell us about them

c/- Weldon Kids, mail box 107, 545 Willoughby Road Willoughby NSW 2068

The Man Behind the Pictures Revealed...

Twenty-six-year-old Sydney artist Jeremy **Andrew** graduated with an architecture degree from Sydney University in 1989, where he was the editor of the newspaper *Honi Soit*. He began drawing for the *Sydney Morning Herald's* "Stay in touch" and "Short black" columns, and in 1992 won the Sydney Opera House 20th Anniversary National Poster Competition, judged from 600 entries by Ken Done. Since 1989 he has had five solo exhibitions of his work, which includes painted surfboards, neon art, furniture design, screen prints, ceramics, paintings and murals. He has recently opened his first shop in Sydney's Surry Hills.

The Owner of this Book Revealed...

The printer threw in some extra pages, so we thought - what a great opportunity for you to make this your own personalised edition.

Name: ....

Name I would have preferred: ....

Nickname(s): ....

....

Address: ....

....

....

Age: ....

Height: ....

Hair colour: ....

Eyes: ....

Favourite sport: ....

Favourite food: ....

Favourite book: .... AUSTRALIA UNCOVERED ....

Number of moles: ....

Number of pets: ....

A picture of me

Trim and paste here

My Personal Records

☐ How many grapes I can put in my mouth without swallowing any.

☐ Distance I can throw an egg.

☐ How many phone numbers I know off by heart.

☐ How many books I've read.

☐ How many peas I can hide under my knife.

☐ How many times I have won the Academy Awards.

☐ How many slices of bread I can balance on my head.

☐ How many times I can run around an oval before collapsing.

What I'd never do when I grow up.

....
....
....
....
....

My Heroes

Sporting...
....
....
....

Movies...
....
....
....

Music...
....
....
....

History...
....
....
....

Other...
....
....
....

If I was Prime Minister, I would make these laws ...

....

....

....

....

....

....

....

....

....

....

....

....

....

....

Places I've Visited in Australia

Name of place: ....Sovereign Hill..........................

Name I think it should be called: ....

....

Date visited (approx.): ....

Comments   ☒ Excellent
                ☐ Good
                ☐ OK
                ☐ Never again

Name of place: Ballarat Wildlife + Reptile Park

Name I think it should be called: ....

....

Date visited (approx.): ....

Comments   ☒ Excellent
                ☐ Good
                ☐ OK
                ☐ Never again

Places I've Visited in Australia

Name of place: Lal Lal Falls

Name I think it should be called: ....

....

Date visited (approx.): ....

Comments
- [ ] Excellent
- [x] Good
- [ ] OK
- [ ] Never again

Name of place: MCG melbourne Cricket Grounds

Name I think it should be called: Melbourne Football Stadium

Date visited (approx.): ....

Comments
- [ ] Excellent
- [x] Good
- [ ] OK
- [ ] Never again

Places I've Visited in Australia

Name of place: _The Twelve Apostles_

Name I think it should be called: ....

....

Date visited (approx.): ....

Comments
☐ Excellent
☐ Good
☐ OK
☐ Never again

Name of place: ....

Name I think it should be called: ....

....

Date visited (approx.): ....

Comments
☐ Excellent
☐ Good
☐ OK
☐ Never again

Places I've Visited in Australia

Name of place: ....

Name I think it should be called: ....

....

Date visited (approx.): ....

Comments ☐ Excellent
☐ Good
☐ OK
☐ Never again

Name of place: ....

Name I think it should be called: ....

....

Date visited (approx.): ....

Comments ☐ Excellent
☐ Good
☐ OK
☐ Never again

Places I've Visited in Australia

Name of place: ....

Name I think it should be called: ....

....

Date visited (approx.): ....

Comments ☐ Excellent
             ☐ Good
             ☐ OK
             ☐ Never again

Name of place: ....

Name I think it should be called: ....

....

Date visited (approx.): ....

Comments ☐ Excellent
             ☐ Good
             ☐ OK
             ☐ Never again
